INTR

Three years ago, Nicholas, my widowed next-door neighbor, sat listening to his children. "You're seventy, Dad, and far too old and set in your ways to change now," they said.

He ignored them and continued to go to polka parties, bingos, and casinos. Then he met a lady and, after a brief courtship, decided to remarry.

After three wonderful years, Nicholas died while on a trip to a city he'd always dreamed of visiting. He fell peacefully into the arms of his wife and smiled as he drew his last breath.

Nothing is more precious than a life fully lived. To live this way is to live with passion—as Nicholas did.

I wrote these reflections because I want you to enjoy life, not just endure it. Take your time reading every day and absorb these pages. Each reflection includes A Simple Reminder, an encouragement to help you live with passion; and A Sincere Request, a prayer to connect you to Jesus.

Lent is a wonderful opportunity for us to stand up to all the cynics who sit in the back row of life, rolling their eyes and whispering negativity and nonsense. To them, we say, "In spite of all the chaos, every day is fresh and full of moments to be savored."

I am honored that you are taking this journey with me. I delight in this precious present moment and bless it by saying, "It's so good to be here."

TWENTY-THIRD PUBLICATIONS A division of Bayard, Inc; 977 Hartford Turnpike Unit A; Waterford, CT 06385
(860) 437-3012 or (800) 321-0411; twentythirdpublications.com

ISBN: 978-1-62785-830-4 • Cover image: © Julia/stock.adobe.com • Printed in the USA

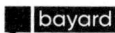

Keep It Simple!

Michael bought a clubhouse for his children. On assembly day, he felt frustrated as each member of his family made a negative comment: "This bolt goes here!" "It doesn't look anything like the picture on the box!" Then Michael learned that he was supposed to tighten all the bolts at least once a month. He didn't own the clubhouse. The clubhouse owned him.

"In praying, do not babble like the pagans, who think that they will be heard because of their many words."

» MATTHEW 6:7

When Jesus sent his disciples out to minister, he told them to take very little. Jesus understood that the simple life was easier to manage.

Today, the distractions we encounter continue to grow and clutter our lives. It's not only the stuff we collect; it's also the unwanted thoughts that nag at the back of our minds—regrets from the past, worries about the future, and all the "should haves" that drain our energy. It's unspoken words that we wish we had said, hurts we continually rehearse, anger and resentment that we keep holding onto, and unresolved family conflicts.

Life is short. Do your best not to miss it.

A Simple Reminder ✳ Make the first day of each month your special day to pamper yourself. Give yourself a day free from heartaches. Throw off your problems. Don't open your mail or pay any bills. Avoid focusing on unpleasant memories, imagined worries, or false fears. Turn off the ringer on your phone so you don't have to listen to people who are critical or complaining. You deserve these bonus days. Give them to yourself.

A Sincere Request ✳ *Dear Jesus, when life gets overwhelming, help me to remember to take time for myself. Amen.*

DEUTERONOMY 30:15-20 • LUKE 9:22-25

Curse It or Carry It

We can't grow unless we're willing to accept delays from life's crosses.

We all have them: an overdue bill that we can't pay, a doctor who tells us, "Nothing more can be done," a spouse who says, "The relationship is over," rebellious children, a major conflict at work. With each cross comes a choice: We can curse it or carry it.

When we curse our cross, we can close down, cling, and compare. When we receive news of a major setback, we can shut people out, withdraw, and avoid returning phone calls. We can cling to unhealthy habits and go overboard eating, drinking, or spending.

"Take up [your] cross and follow me."

» LUKE 9:23

We look at other people and compare ourselves by asking, "Why did this happen to me? I'm a good person. What did I do wrong?"

When we persistently curse our cross, we sentence ourselves to a life of anger, bitterness, and resentment.

When we carry our cross, however, we can accept, align, and ask.

Accept what's going on in our lives. Let go of resistance.

Align with an outcome that will bring relief. Focus on that outcome and find thoughts that help us feel better.

Then, ask for help. Trust that God will give us the wisdom and strength to make the changes that we're able to make. When we don't have control, trust that God will help us move through the experience.

A Simple Reminder ✳ Create and Carry. Make a list of things to be grateful for. Carry that list with you during Lent as a gentle reminder.

A Sincere Request ✳ *Dear Jesus, help me carry this cross, be grateful for my life, and feel relief. Amen.*

Nothing Lasts Forever

One day two widowers meet in a cemetery. Each man is crying over the grave of his wife. Each is tearful, but clearly, one is more upset than the other.

The first man cries, "I loved her so much. She was so wonderful, kind, and loving. She was everything to me."

The second man says, "So was my dear wife."

"But you don't understand," the first man says. "She was my whole life!"

"So was mine," the second man replies.

"The days will come when the bridegroom is taken away from them."

» MATTHEW 9:15

Then the first man, with anguish in his eyes, screams, "No, you don't understand—I never told her!"

"The bridegroom will not always be with us"—but we often live as if we have all the time in the world. Then, without warning, our lives are turned upside down by illness, loss, or death. And all we can do is look back with regret, wondering why we didn't express our appreciation, care for someone in need, spend more time with our children, or just say, "I love you."

As long as we have life, we have new opportunities. Since we have limited time, make that time count. Tell your loved ones now how you feel.

A Simple Reminder ✳ What opportunities does God bring to your attention? Be still for a moment. Then write them down. Decide to take action, even if it seems impossible.

A Sincere Request ✳ *Dear Jesus, when opportunity knocks, nudge me to answer the door immediately. Amen.*

Isaiah 58:9b–14 • Luke 5:27–32

What's Next?

My friend Teresa's life is a litany of heartaches. Her husband had a gambling problem. After his death, she discovered piles of debt. Foreclosure of their home followed. Her son sits in a Florida jail after committing armed robbery and murder. Her daughter is high most of the time and overdoses regularly.

> *"Those who are healthy do not need a physician, but the sick do."*
>
> » LUKE 5:31

"After the initial shocks," Teresa said, "I found a way to manage my anger. I could have isolated myself, obsessed over what happened, and cried out to God in despair. Instead, I picked myself up and moved ahead. I chose to refuse one path and find refuge in another."

When life challenges you with a problem, refuse and find refuge:

- Refuse to listen to people who remind you of your past trauma. Turn off the movie inside your head that replays your hurt over and over.
- Refuge is where you can rebound, regain your strength, build your confidence, and rendezvous with Jesus, who wants to heal us. Your refuge can be a private location or an understanding person with whom you feel safe enough to share your feelings. From this place of relief, you can slowly let go of your hurts and ask, "What's next?"

A Simple Reminder ✳ Write these words on a piece of paper: "Jesus, please help me with this." Tape the paper to a door in your home. Whenever you experience one of life's hurts, write it down on this piece of paper. Then, once a week, shred the paper, let go of the hurts, and get on with your life.

A Sincere Request ✳ *Dear Jesus, help me let go of my hurts and move forward. Amen.*

Keep Moving Forward!

Life goes along and then, all of a sudden, the bottom falls out. In these times, it's easy to feel despair. We want to crawl into bed and disappear.

Despair is a devastating emotion that drains our energy. As hard as we may try to avoid it, it's important to know what to do if we experience it. Surprisingly, the answer is simple: Just keep moving forward!

> *"You shall not put the Lord, your God, to the test." When the devil had finished every temptation, he departed.*
>
> » LUKE 4:12-13

We can learn a lesson from Jesus' desert duel with the devil: The worst thing we can do is focus on the anguish that we're experiencing. Jesus' anguish came in three strong waves of temptations, but Jesus kept moving forward. We need to do the same.

Edmund Burke, a British statesman and philosopher, said, "Never despair; but if you do, work on in despair." This advice is about as simple as it gets. Don't stop pursuing your dreams and goals. Don't forget the reason why you started your journey, whatever it may be. Get out of bed and start moving!

A Simple Reminder ✳ If you've had a tragic event in your life, what thoughts could bring a measure of relief? What do you have to be grateful for? What have you accomplished in your life? Write it down.

If you've lost a job, brainstorm new ways to earn the revenue you need. What are you naturally good at? What do you do in your spare time that you enjoy? Keep your mind open and allow the ideas to flow. Brainstorm with your family and a few close friends.

A Sincere Request ✳ *Dear Jesus, when I'm faced with a hopeless situation, help me feel better and move forward. Amen.*

LEVITICUS 19:1-2, 11-18 • MATTHEW 25:31-46

Just Do It!

When her baby died, Sheila became a recluse. Two women from her parish were determined to bring joy and hope back into her life. They invited Sheila to be their guest at a Josh Groban concert. She resisted. They persisted. In the end, she accepted and enjoyed herself for the first time in months. She was finally able to feel her heart again.

> *"Amen, I say to you, whatever you did for one of these least brothers of mine, you did for me.."*
>
> » MATTHEW 25:40

Many people are so hurt and wounded that they need a lot of kindness and gentleness. You could be the one who makes a difference in their lives.

Kindness begets kindness. Every act of kindness builds us up and strengthens our spirit. People respond favorably. Sometimes, an act of kindness can create such an impact that the person remembers it for the rest of his or her life. Perhaps you will remember it too.

As members of the church community, we need to continue the work of Jesus and seek out people who are broken, scared, or shy. We need to look for overworked, overlooked, and overwrought people and give them a dose of kindness. Opportunities like this are everywhere. Seize the moment!

A Simple Reminder ✳ Try to do little things that will help someone have a better day. There are many random acts of kindness that you could do: Buy a meal for the person behind you at a drive-through. Smile and say "Hi" to a passing stranger. Pay someone a compliment. Kindness is contagious. Keep it going!

A Sincere Request ✳ *Dear Jesus, I want to be kind. Help me get started. Amen.*

Get Out of the Way!

While shopping in a grocery store, I spotted a woman walking toward me with her arms full of empty boxes. She bumped into everyone and everything as she slowly made her way down the aisle. Suddenly, she found herself wedged between the boxes and a shelf. With a sigh, she looked at me and said, "I seem to be getting in my own way."

"Our Father in heaven, hallowed be your name."

» MATTHEW 6:9

I often find myself saying similar words to people: "You need to get out of your own way." Most of us (including yours truly) are guilty of getting in our own way from time to time.

Have you ever noticed how some of us try to become what others want us to be? We create disguises and hide behind them. The person we're hiding (just to fit in) is blocked. We get in our own way.

Be sure of this: You are privileged, precious, and priceless in God's eyes. So, avoid those who undermine you and leave you feeling depressed and defeated. Tune them out and turn them off.

You are all you have. Therefore, see yourself as the most beautiful, wonderful, fantastic person you can be.

A Simple Reminder ✳ On the back of some index cards, write down statements such as "I love myself just the way I am," "I am somebody," or "I am a child of God." Give the cards to people who need to accept and experience their own true magnificence. Encourage them to repeat the statements several times each day. Oh, and keep a card for yourself.

A Sincere Request ✳ *Dear Jesus, help me remove all the obstacles that get in the way of my knowing my magnificence. Amen.*

JONAH 3:1-10 • LUKE 11:29-32

Anything Is Possible

After spending months in recovery to get her life back, Margaret used her own life experience to find her passion: She started a recovery group for woman with addictions.

Want to find your passion? Then release your negative thoughts. Negative thinking causes more negative thinking. Fear produces anxiety. Anxiety leads to insecurity. Soon, you're in a cycle—creating your own limitations and accepting them as real.

> *"At the preaching of Jonah they repented, and there is something greater than Jonah here."*
>
> » LUKE 11:32

Many people cling to past mistakes and struggles. They become overwhelmed, not only from the critical and condemning comments of others but from their own negative thoughts. Stop listening to those voices!

Your past is not your future. Release limiting thoughts and realize your potential. Believe in yourself—what you can do and who you can become.

The power to improve your life is in your hands. Just make the decision to change. If the desire to move forward is strong enough, you can do it. The predominant thought is—"I can!" The words are—"I will!" Our greatest need is to believe that anything is possible.

A Simple Reminder ✳ Practice repetition. Experts say that it takes twenty-one days for a change in behavior to become a habit and a minimum of six months for the practice to become ingrained into your daily life. Begin your positive habits now.

....

A Sincere Request ✳ *Dear Jesus, I can overcome my perceived limitations. With your help, I will be free to live a productive and joyful life. Amen.*

9

ESTHER C:12, 14–16, 23–25 • MATTHEW 7:7-12

Don't Worry, Be Happy!

Many of us believe that worrying about something is not going to change the outcome. One gentleman, however, doesn't agree. He was lying on the couch talking to his therapist and said, "Worrying works for me. Ninety-nine percent of the things I worry about never happen."

> *"Ask and it will be given to you."*
> » MATTHEW 7:7

If you're like me, you probably believe this, too—worry about it and it won't happen. Whenever something unexpected occurs, we tend to start worrying about the worst possible scenario.

Wouldn't it be nice if we could take all of our worries and just not worry about them anymore—just be happy? We can.

When life hits us and so many things can go wrong, the remedy is not to worry yourself sick but to relinquish worry through prayer.

Pray about what's really in your heart. Pray about everything (no exceptions). In other words, there is no problem, no circumstance, and no situation that cannot be brought before God.

Accept the invitation of Jesus to "ask" and then trust Jesus will fill your need or mend your hurt. Prayer is a meaningful conversation with God. Ask for guidance. Request to be led to the perfect person who can help you!

A Simple Reminder ✳ Friends can give you a different perspective, but there's a caveat here: Be sure you pick people who have control over their own worries. Find someone who can listen and offer positive and constructive support.

A Sincere Request ✳ *Dear Jesus, it's time to open my heart and let go of the worry. I trust that you'll help me when I ask. Amen.*

Ezekiel 18:21-28 • Matthew 5:20-26

Just Let Go!

For years, my friend Barbara felt a deep resentment toward Marge, who had betrayed their friendship. Then, one day, she heard that Marge was dying of cancer. Time was running out. She rushed to Marge's home and begged her forgiveness for staying away so long. Both women burst into tears as their raw feelings came pouring out.

> *"Leave your gift there at the altar, go first and be reconciled."*
>
> » MATTHEW 5:24

Most of us have had people in our lives who have hurt us. If, years later, we still haven't forgiven them, the resentment will eat away at us—not at them. Most likely, they won't care or even be aware of our feelings. So, we are the only ones who will suffer.

If we can't forgive a person, then he or she still has control over us. Regardless of who was at fault, or how right we thought we were in defending ourselves, we will carry that pain until we're able to let go.

Forgiveness is not about letting the other person off the hook or excusing their hurtful behavior. Instead, it's about letting go of the emotional attachment to their actions, especially the feelings of anger and bitterness.

A Simple Reminder ✳ If you're having a difficult time with forgiveness, try writing down these words: "I forgive (person's name) for hurting me."

Speak these words over and over again. Don't stop until you feel the shift inside. Don't stop until you really mean it.

A Sincere Request ✳ *Dear Jesus, help me let go of past hurts and move on with my life. Amen.*

DEUTERONOMY 26:16–19 • MATTHEW 5:43–48

Respond with Understanding

Do difficult people feel they have a mission from God? Do they hear God saying, "Your ultimate work in life is to be difficult; do everything in your power to irritate others; be irresponsible, demanding, negative, selfish, and angry"?

> *"Love your enemies, and pray for those who persecute you."*
>
> » MATTHEW 5:44

Many of us have had to deal with difficult people in our lives. Since they refuse to change, we cannot allow them to draw us into their world of yelling, screaming, spewing insults, or using intimidation. When this happens, they've got us. We're now operating on their level.

The key to dealing with people like this is to take responsibility. We are absolutely accountable for how we treat others; but we are not to blame for how they treat us. We can, however, control our reaction to their behavior.

The next time someone upsets you, try the advice of Jesus: "Love your enemies!" Then respond with understanding and compassion. Often, they're hurting inside. Don't allow their words to get to you. Breathe deeply and remember that they are children of God.

Try to put yourself in their place. You're not excusing their offensive behavior, but since you may understand where it comes from, you won't have to take it so personally.

A Simple Reminder ✳ Pick your difficult people wisely. Spend time with someone who is irritable or impossible to deal with. Respond with understanding and compassion. Help them find a true sense of self-worth.

A Sincere Request ✳ *Dear Jesus, help me to understand, respond with love, and experience the good in everyone. Amen.*

GENESIS 15:5-12, 17-18 • PHILIPPIANS 3:17—4:1 *or* 3:20—4:1 • LUKE 9:28B-36

Look Inside!

A beggar had been sitting by the side of the road for many years. One day, as a stranger walked by, the beggar asked him for spare change.

"What's that you're sitting on?" the stranger asked.

"Just an old box that I've been using for as long as I can remember."

"Ever look inside?"

"No. What's the point? There's nothing in there." But the stranger insisted.

> *"It is good that we are here."*
> » LUKE 9:33

The beggar managed to pry open the lid, and with astonishment and joy he discovered that the box was filled with gold.

We, too, are sitting on gold. If we look inside ourselves, we will discover that we have our own fortune of uniqueness, value, and worth. For some of us, though, that person is covered with layers of self-doubt and feelings of inadequacy. These layers have accumulated from listening too long to people who tell us we aren't good enough, pretty enough, or smart enough.

It doesn't matter what anyone else thinks—God sees us as remarkable human beings. There's nothing we can do to make God love us more, or less.

Look inside yourself. You'll come to know, be, and love yourself as God loves you. And you will be saying, like Peter, "It's good to be here."

A Simple Reminder ✳ Make a list of everything you love about yourself: I am an excellent cook, parent, spouse, child. I am compassionate. Contemplate each item on the list and say, "Yes, I am blessed to have this quality, and it will be with me for the rest of my life."

A Sincere Request ✳ *Dear Jesus, help me to see myself from the inside out and embrace my uniqueness. Amen.*

DANIEL 9:4B–10 • LUKE 6:36–38

No Judging Allowed!

It happens in every moment of every day. It could be the weather conditions, the taste of our food, a television program, our bank account, or our neighbor's car. Whatever it is, our natural tendency is to judge.

> *"Stop judging and you will not be judged."*
>
> » LUKE 6:37

Most of us are quick to form an opinion about everyone and everything. We particularly make immediate judgments about people.

When we are quick to judge others, because of something they said, or the job they did, or their hairstyle, or their age, or any number of other reasons, we fail to see the real person. It causes a triple consequence: our loss, their loss, and the loss of a community where people are valued and respected.

When we quickly "sum up" another person, it prevents us from seeing the goodness that lies below the surface and beyond his or her appearance.

We cannot judge another unless we've arrived in his or her place. And since we can never be in exactly the same place and life circumstance as another person, Jesus is clear—"Stop judging."

Dwelling excessively on our judgments can hurt us. We may be angry or frustrated because people don't do what we think they should do. We must learn that other people aren't here to do what we want; they're here to do what they're called to do.

A Simple Reminder ✳ Try to see through the eyes of Jesus. We all know people who feel passed over, forgotten, dismissed, or judged. Let them know you care. Take time to get acquainted. Pay them a compliment. Do something special for them.

A Sincere Request ✳ *Dear Jesus, I'm responsible for my life and my actions. Help me be more accepting of others. Amen.*

ISAIAH 1:10, 16–20 • **MATTHEW 23:1–12**

Stop It!

I once knew a woman who had just about everything a person could want. Besides being beautiful, she was well educated, wealthy, and generous.

But even with all her fine qualities, she was miserable. At times she was so deeply depressed that she even thought of ending her life. How did she get into that sad state? By listening to the comments of critical people. She tried to win their approval. She lived in fear that if she didn't measure up to their expectations, she would never be good enough, and thus, never be loved.

> *"For they preach but they do not practice."*
>
> » MATTHEW 23:3

What happened to this wonderful woman? I'm happy to say that she finally learned how to deal with her critics. She found the courage to say, "I'll listen to your opinion, but from now on, I won't let you rule my life."

Do you ever let critical people get the best of you? They're all around us. These people can cause us to feel guilty, ashamed, or incompetent, if we let them. They usually operate under the guise of helping us. Jesus encountered critical people, and he knew "they don't practice what they preach."

Whether we work with them, or live with them, critical people can make life difficult. These SOPs—Sources of Pain—are a major cause of our frustration, anger, and resentment. They will continue to affect us until we stand on our own two feet, look them straight in the eye and say, "Stop it!"

A Simple Reminder ✳ It is surprising how a kind word or expression of praise can improve our relationships. The next time someone criticizes you, simply offer them a compliment and see what happens.

A Sincere Request ✳ *Dear Jesus, give me the courage to stand up to all the critics and say, "Enough!" Amen.*

15

2 SAMUEL 7:4–5A, 12–14A, 16 • ROMANS 4:13, 16–18, 22 • MATTHEW 1:16, 18–21, 24A
or LUKE 2:41–51A

The Language of Dreams

Mary stops by Joseph's carpenter shop and drops the bomb—she's pregnant! Devastated and disappointed, Joseph finds himself wrestling with a dilemma: How am I going to get out of this relationship?

An angel of the Lord appeared to him in a dream...

» MATTHEW 1:20

During sleep that night, he has a dream that changes the direction of his life. It brings him face to face with his problem, reduces his fear, lessens his anguish, provides insight into his situation, and points to a solution.

Dreams can help us glean important information about who we are and what we want out of life. Consider keeping a dream journal and a pen next to your bed for early-morning scribbles. When you wake up, take a few minutes to capture your dream. Then, ask yourself: Are there any unfinished issues in my relationships? Do I constantly recount past sufferings, fears, or anxieties? What really pushes my buttons? What fences need mending? What concerns am I not able to handle? Are there any associations, however subtle, that can be connected to my dream?

It may take a while to connect all of your fragmented parts through dream journaling. Just keep writing. Work on the issues that challenge you so you can experience joy, courage, faith, wisdom, and peace.

A Simple Reminder ✳ Read the dreams of Jacob (Genesis 28:10–28) and Joseph (Genesis 37:1–11). Review your dream journal and ask: How is God nudging me, through my dreams, to change my life?

··

A Sincere Request ✳ *Dear Jesus, speak to me in my dreams. I am ready to listen. Amen.*

JEREMIAH 17:5-10 • LUKE 16:19-31

If Only I Had Known!

As Betty stood on the street corner, she noticed a young girl standing on the opposite curb, crying. When the traffic light changed, Betty and the girl started walking across the street toward each other. Just as they were about to cross paths, Betty's motherly instincts took over. Every part of her being wanted to reach out and comfort that girl. But for some reason, she kept walking. Days later, those tear-filled eyes continued to haunt her.

> *"And lying at his door was a poor man named Lazarus."*
>
> » LUKE 16:20

"Why didn't I offer to help?" she asked. "Only a few seconds would have been enough time to let her know that someone cared. Instead, I did nothing." With a little effort the rich man in our gospel story could have reached out and helped Lazarus, but he chose to ignore him.

God has fine-tuned us to go out and give generously. But too often we say, "If there's anything I can do, just let me know." Instead of waiting for someone to ask for assistance, we need to make the initial effort to connect. Someone needs a hug today. Someone needs a smile. Someone needs a friend. Find those people and offer to help.

Use Lent to work on being more helpful and feeling less regret. The saddest words ever spoken are "If only I had known!"

A Simple Reminder ✳ Human touch is a miracle drug. Look for those who are distressed, overwhelmed, or unappreciated, and offer them a hug!

A Sincere Request ✳ *Dear Jesus, help me give to others the love and compassion that I need for myself. Amen.*

GENESIS 37:3-4, 12-13A, 17B-28A • **MATTHEW 21:33-43, 45-46**

I Have Value!

The honeymoon was over. Andrea was now dealing with her husband's snide remarks. He would frequently bombard her with critical comments about her appearance, her opinions, and more.

> *"This is the heir. Come, let us kill him and acquire his inheritance."*
>
> » MATTHEW 21:38

I'll never forget her response: "If I'm so awful, why did you marry me?"

Few things are more destructive than the casual putdown. We can become so accustomed to it that we fail to realize how devastating it can be.

Ralph Waldo Emerson spoke of a simple weed as "a plant whose virtues have not yet been discovered." How many people have we written off as weeds because they appeared unworthy of our attention? We can be like the tenants in the gospel who had no respect for the landowner's son.

Like others, we too can feel the effect of ridicule. If we allow those remarks to continue, they will chisel away at our self-esteem. We must make the commitment to listen only to those who empower us. We need to stand up for ourselves and say those magical words: I have value!

A Simple Reminder ✳ If you are being ridiculed, claim your power and speak up! If, however, you have a tendency to ridicule others, try this: Buy a bag of marbles. Every time you catch yourself making a negative comment about someone, put a marble in a cup. See how many marbles you collect by Easter and then donate a dollar for each to your favorite charity.

A Sincere Request ✳ *Dear Jesus, when I open my mouth, may my words lift people rather than level them. Amen.*

MICAH 7:14-15, 18-20 • LUKE 15:1-3, 11-32

Tongue Tied?

Do you sometimes have difficulty expressing words that get caught between your good intentions and your fear of rejection? You're not alone!

Take, for example, those two seldom heard words, "I'm sorry."

"Father, I have sinned against heaven and against you."
» LUKE 15:18

Those words don't assign blame. Instead, they tend to make things right. For many of us, though, saying "I'm sorry" is a painful admission of fault—a belief that we possess some weakness or vulnerability.

The exact opposite is true. Being able to say "I was wrong" is one of the surest signs of strength we can have. Our ability to apologize shows that we are sensitive to the pain of others. Saying "I'm sorry" is far better than putting up walls or trying to maintain the myth that we're perfect. Those two magical words have the unlimited power to heal and restore.

The prodigal son rehearsed his "I'm sorry" all the way home. I don't suppose he traveled very fast. But we read that his father ran. Slow are the steps of repentance, but swift are the feet of forgiveness.

His father "ran to his son, embraced him, and kissed him"—kissed him eagerly. He did not delay a moment; for though he was out of breath, he was not out of love.

A Simple Reminder ✳ During Lent, plan a meal with friends and talk about what it means to be together. Tell them how you feel.

A Sincere Request ✳ *Dear Jesus, thank you for the love you give me through my family and friends. Help me share it with those I meet. Amen.*

19

EXODUS 3:1–8A, 13–15 • 1 CORINTHIANS 10:1–6, 10–12 • LUKE 13:1–9
FOR YEAR A: EXODUS 17:3–7 • ROMANS 5:1–2, 5–8 • JOHN 4:5–42 *or* 4:5–15, 19B–26, 39A, 40–42

Stay at It!

Meet Gene. He's lived through four wars, the Great Depression, ninety winters, and who knows how many personal hardships. Yet, at ninety years of age, he still embraces life. Ask him his secret and he'll say, "Stay at it."

Adversity is inevitable. Terrible things often happen, with severe consequences. Our hardships can have one of two outcomes: They can defeat us or they can develop us. It all depends on how we respond to them.

"It may bear fruit in the future."
» LUKE 13:9

We could blow our difficulties out of proportion. We could surrender and allow anguish and depression to overwhelm us.

Here's another choice: Contemplate. Ask for guidance and strength. Rather than throwing your hands up in despair, lift them up in prayer. Jesus will answer, "Stay at it." He'll provide courage, patience, and support.

Jesus helps us see the hidden secrets within our traumas, the promised blessings yet to come. Ask yourself: What lesson am I learning from this? Even if it's a difficult lesson, consider what it has taught you and how much you have grown.

A Simple Reminder ✳ Think about a stonecutter, hammering away at his rock. He strikes it perhaps a hundred times before seeing as much as a crack. Yet, at the 101st blow, the rock splits in two. It wasn't the last blow that caused the rock to break open, but all that chiseling that happened before. Likewise, it's not our final actions that resolve our problems, but our moment-by-moment responses to them as they unfold. Will you crumble or, like Gene, will you stay at it?

A Sincere Request ✳ *Dear Jesus, encourage me to always stay the course and never give up. Amen.*

2 KINGS 5:1-15AB • LUKE 4:24-30

Hope Is in the House!

You've heard the saying "Don't get your hopes up." Well, I want to tell you just the opposite: Do get your hopes up, because hope is in the house, and it has a name—Jesus!

Jesus connected with people whose lives were at an all-time low: a woman caught in adultery; Zacchaeus, who was a crook; a woman who had been married five times; the paralyzed and the possessed; all hanging on by a thread and ready to let go. Jesus entered their world and said, "Don't you dare give up! Anchor yourself in me and connect with others."

> *"No prophet is accepted in his own native place."*
>
> » LUKE 4:24

In the midst of despair, we can look away from our problems and turn our focus to Jesus. What are those inner messages that we receive on a daily basis? What is the lesson that he wants to teach us?

We can ask, "What am I supposed to do?" The answer is simple: Do what Jesus did—connect with people who will invite you into their lives and accept you as you are—unlike the hometown folks Jesus encountered in our gospel today. Look for hope in the right faces. Form one-on-one relationships and say, "I care. I understand. You've had a bad day? Let's talk."

A Simple Reminder ✳ Commit yourself to being an encourager—a hope-bringer. Look around you and take note of your friends who are depressed and ready to give up. Pick up the phone and say, "You haven't been yourself lately. It's time that we talk."

A Sincere Request ✳ *Dear Jesus, keep helping me through the tough times when my face is in the dust. I'm putting all my problems in your hands. How much safer could I be? Thank you for loving me. Amen.*

ISAIAH 7:10-14; 8:10 • HEBREWS 10:4-10 • LUKE 1:26-38

Be Courageously Dependent!

Luke's gospel begins with an "impossible" mission brought to Mary. But there's just one problem with that mission: Mary isn't married. She asks, "How can this be?"

We may ask that same question when we have no solution for a tragedy or problem. During these times, we need to turn it all over to God.

"Nothing will be impossible with God."

» LUKE 1:37

Instead of running away, complaining, or holding a pity party, say, "God, nothing is too difficult for you. Help me!"

Next, try this exercise:

Think of the impossible situation that is weighing you down. Get scraps of paper and write down different aspects of your problem. When you have described each element, seal all the scraps of paper in an envelope.

With both hands, lift up the envelope. Tell God about your situation and voice your feelings of anger, doubt, frustration, and fear.

Keep that envelope in the air until the pain in your arms is equal to the pain in your heart. Then, drop your arms and say, "God, take it."

Place the envelope in a safe place and continue living your life.

Reaffirm your commitment to God. Believe, with all your heart, that everything will be OK.

A Simple Reminder ✳ Who do you go to when facing an impossible situation? Make a list and put "God" at the top.

....

A Sincere Request ✳ *Dear Jesus, you specialize in impossible situations. I am so grateful for your solutions. Help me act on them. Amen.*

Anchors Aweigh!

When I was a first-year high school religion teacher, I stopped going to the teachers' lounge. Besides the haze of cigarette smoke that drifted through the room, there was a deep cloud of emotional negativity present.

> *"But whoever obeys and teaches these commandments will be called greatest in the kingdom."*
> » MATTHEW 5:19

There are two types of people: Anchors and Motors.

Anchors keep us chained to our past. They find fault with everyone and everything. They judge, complain, blame, and pull us down. They walk into a room and drain us of our energy and enthusiasm. Don't allow Anchor-people to deplete your self-esteem by reminding you of who you could have been or what you could have done.

Motors are just the opposite. They remind us of our strengths. They are positive, nourishing, and uplifting. They believe in us and encourage us to learn from our mistakes, applaud our victories, and pursue our dreams. When we stumble, they are always there to remind us of how far we've come.

Choose to be a Motor. You will be great in the kingdom of heaven.

A Simple Reminder ✳ Make a list of everyone you spend time with on a regular basis. Classify them as either Anchors or Motors. Decide to free yourself from the Anchor-people in your life. And, if that's not possible, then dramatically decrease the amount of time you spend with them.

....

A Sincere Request ✳ *Dear Jesus, surround me with those who lift me up. Help me look at everyone with understanding and see their inner beauty and worth as God's children. Amen.*

JEREMIAH 7:23–28 • LUKE 11:14–23

I Have a Dream!

Some people have a clear sense of their own destiny. In the movie *Simon Birch*, a young boy (with stunted growth) believes he was placed on Earth to be "God's instrument." He's convinced that he's going to be a hero, although he isn't quite sure how. He says, "God made me the way I am for a reason" and "God has a dream for everyone."

> *"When a strong man fully armed guards his palace, his possessions are safe."*
> » LUKE 11:21

As we reach for our dreams, we will encounter those who will ridicule, sabotage, and discount our efforts. Simon Birch did, and what a lesson he taught us! It's the same lesson we hear in our reading today—be fully armed against any attackers. When people made fun of Simon, he simply looked at them, smiled, and said, "Have a nice day." He was aware of his greater purpose. He knew his destiny! Simon certainly was prepared.

You, too, can know your destiny. Keep your dreams alive by visualizing a special three-rung ladder. The first rung is determination. The second is dedication, and the third is attitude. Pursue your goals one step at a time. Find people to support you and, while you're at it, help others achieve their dreams along the way.

A Simple Reminder ✳ Schedule a movie night with friends. Rent or stream the movie *Simon Birch*, then share your dreams with one another. Be sure to keep a box of tissues nearby.

A Sincere Request ✳ *Dear Jesus, I know you have big plans for me, and I'm determined to achieve them. Please help me. Amen.*

Saved by the Light!

Some people refuse to let tragedy overwhelm them. Instead, they find a sense of purpose in their lives and the strength to move on. They follow the light.

The world needs compassionate Candle-lighters to pick up those who have been knocked down by bad news. Life's terrible experiences have the triple-whammy effect of pain, worry, and self-doubt. They can leave us feeling desolate and wondering if we'll ever see the light

"You shall love your neighbor as yourself."
» MARK 12:31

again. At these times, Candle-lighters can shine their inner guidance and help us deal with the crisis until we find relief from our worry and pain.

Having fumbled in the dark themselves, Candle-lighters have earned "been there before" credentials. They've been fine-tuned by the Holy Spirit to be more compassionate, more caring, more loving, more concerned, and more aware of the pain of others.

Candle-lighters invite the Holy Spirit into their hearts to guide them through the darkness of despair into the light of hope; giving comfort, calming fear, and helping to carry the burden for those of us who are feeling hurt, frightened, and alone.

A Simple Reminder ✳ Become a Candle-lighter. Shine that ray of hope for others. Purchase neon 3 x 5 index cards. On the front, write out the words of Philippians 4:8. Tape a tiny candle to the back of the card. Mail them to those who are stuck in a dark place.

A Sincere Request ✳ *Dear Jesus, your light is shining strongly. As a Candle-lighter, with your help I will embrace it and direct it toward others. Amen.*

The Rest of the Story!

I wish we could hear the rest of this story. Both of these men must have experienced tremendous change. Did the tax collector get a new job? Was he more accepted? Did he make amends to the people? What about the Pharisee? Did he live up to his reputation? Did he become more spiritual?

> *"Two people went up to the temple area to pray: one was a Pharisee and the other was a tax collector."*
>
> » LUKE 18:10

We don't know the rest of their stories. It doesn't matter. What does matter is the rest of *our* story. The one thing that most of us want, need, and fear the most is change. The process can be frightening. The question to ask is this: When it comes to change, am I a Talker or a Doer?

Talkers end up stuck in the same ruts. They ramble on and on about change, yet never get around to it.

Doers know their lives have been out of control. They take action to create a better life. It may be difficult, and it may take them in a totally new direction. Like the tax collector and the Pharisee, Doers become an inspiration to others, reminding us, "If I can change, so can you."

God is calling us to live, respond, grow, improve, and change. Decide to be a Doer and watch remarkable new adventures unfold in your life.

A Simple Reminder ✴ Name your rut: feeling impatience, experiencing anger, demanding the need to be right, holding onto grudges, or brooding over injuries. It's time to let go. Talk to Jesus and tell him your plans for changing your life. Write down your ideas for being happier, healthier, more creative, and more successful.

A Sincere Request ✴ *Dear Jesus, remind me that change starts with two words: "I can." With your help, I will. Amen.*

JOSHUA 5:9A, 10-12 • 2 CORINTHIANS 5:17-21 • LUKE 15:1-3, 11-32
FOR YEAR A: 1 SAMUEL 16:1B, 6-7, 10-13A • EPHESIANS 5:8-14 • JOHN 9:1-41
or 9:1, 6-9, 13-17, 34-38

Leave No Room for Envy!

Envy sneaks up on us when we least expect it. If we allow it to con-
sume us, it can destroy a marriage, ruin a career, and alienate friends.
It can suck the joy right out of our lives.

The father in today's parable sees how envy
is ruining his older son's life. He wants to free
him from how it is hurting him, so he tries to
dissuade him from his envious rage by explain-
ing, "You are always with me—and everything
I have is yours."

Envy-free people appreciate what they
already have. Ask them what they need, and
they'll say, "Not much."

It's different with the envious. Jealousy
starts gnawing at their hearts. They completely
overlook their own good fortune and become
obsessed with other people's possessions, popularity, and lifestyle.

*"But when
your son
returns who
swallowed
up your
property with
prostitutes,
for him you
slaughter the
fattened calf."*

» LUKE 15:30

What can we do to let go of envy? We can redirect our attention
from someone else's life to our own, from what we don't have to what
we do have, from where we've failed to where we've succeeded, from
lack-consciousness to prosperity-consciousness. This kind of mind-
set leaves no room for envy.

A Simple Reminder ✳ Create your own bucket of blessings. Each
day, write out on index cards the good things in your life and what
you are grateful for. Then, drop the cards into your bucket. Reread
them each week to remind you of how wonderful your life is and how
blessed you already are.

A Sincere Request ✳ *Dear Jesus, remind me to appreciate
the blessings that you lovingly send my way. Amen.*

The Comfort of Silence

"Your kids are all you think about," Barbara said as we sat next to her son's bedside at hospice. Through tears, she expressed her intense grief at the prospect of losing her child. She could relate to the royal official's desperate need for Jesus to come help him.

The royal official said to him, "Sir, come down before my child dies."
» JOHN 4:49

At times like these, we want to help, but we don't know how. Our words may be more discouraging than encouraging. The last thing we want to do is hurt those who are grieving. So, what do we say? And what don't we say?

Don't say, "You're still young. You can have another child someday." Another child will not replace the one who died.

Don't say, "I know how you feel." Unless you've lost a child of your own, you cannot possibly imagine what they are going through.

Don't say, "Your child is in heaven now." It doesn't matter where the child is. All that matters is that their child is no longer here!

So, what do you say? Nothing. Instead of sharing empty words, be a silent presence and show that you care. Let them cry, yell, complain, or talk endlessly about how much they loved their child.

Our compassionate presence will help them along the way.

A Simple Reminder ✳ Many people show up at a funeral, offer support, and then disappear. Grieving parents need us most when everyone else is gone. During the first week or two, they may be oblivious to their surroundings. Reality is going to hit, and hit hard. They're going to need you more than ever. Be there for them.

A Sincere Request ✳ *Dear Jesus, during these times, help me to be a strong, compassionate, loving presence who offers the comfort of silence. Amen.*

28

Respond Now or Regret Later

Anthony stood in the cold, watching people go in and out of the department store. His coat barely fit him; the front was fastened together with safety pins, and his shoes were held together with duct tape.

> *"Sir, I have no one to put me in the pool when the water is stirred up."*
> » JOHN 5:7

A woman saw Anthony as she entered the store. A little later she came out, walked up to him, and said, "Try this coat on—it may be your size." He put it on and said, "Oh, it's so nice and warm." Then she handed him gloves and shoes. He took them and then, stunned by his good fortune, he thanked her and said, "Lady, are you God's wife?"

She smiled, laughed, and said, "No, I'm just one of God's children."

Anthony's face lit up. "I knew it! I knew you were related!"

God's children hear the call for help and respond by filling needs and mending hurts. They work at "making time" to be attentive. Unlike the people in our gospel today who distanced themselves from the man, treating him like he was part of the landscape, God's children ask, "How can I help?"

Begin small. Share a smile and give an encouraging word. Then, work up to the big stuff.

A Simple Reminder ✳ Troubled souls are all around us. It takes courage to walk up to strangers and offer to help. Get clear about your intention. Use your intuition. Approach them in a safe place. Ask someone to go with you. Connect heart to heart before you make contact. People with needs and hurts are right in front of us. Keep your eyes open and offer support.

A Sincere Request ✳ *Dear Jesus, help me recognize those who need my help. Amen.*

What Would You Say?

Dr. Randy Pausch was a talented professor. His world took an unexpected turn when pancreatic cancer came back into his life with a vengeance.

On September 8, 2007, he delivered his "Last Lecture." He announced that he wasn't there to talk about death or to ask for pity, but to talk about Achieving Your Childhood Dreams and the Importance of Living.

> *"Whoever hears my word and believes in the one who sent me has eternal life."*
>
> » JOHN 5:24

Like Randy, we all know that we're going to die someday, but many of us act as if it will never happen. The certainty of death is a reminder to:

- *Let Go.* Why worry about all the stuff you've accumulated? You can't take it with you.
- *Show Love.* I've never read the obituary of a person who died from an overdose of hugs or kisses. We don't have forever. Love now.
- *Celebrate Life.* The tragedy is to reach the end of your life without ever having really lived.

When Jesus calls us home, we're not going to need eyeglasses, hearing aids, or credit cards. If we take action now, we'll be content then, knowing that we did all the things we wanted to do, saw all the places we wanted to see, and said all the words we wanted to say.

A Simple Reminder ✳ If you had one last lecture or message to give before you died, what would you say?

A Sincere Request ✳ *Dear Jesus, when I come home, this life will become a distant memory. Help me focus on the important things. Amen.*

EXODUS 32:7-14 • JOHN 5:31-47

Stop Complaining!

We all know what it's like to be around someone who complains a lot. We'd be wise to limit our contact with them because complaining can be contagious. It prolongs our unhappiness and infects those around us.

"John was a burning and shining lamp, and for a while you were content to rejoice in his light."

» JOHN 5:35

Will Bowen, a Kansas City minister, wants to create a Complaint Free World. "It is one thing to say 'change your thoughts' and it's another to realize what you're thinking," he says. "Just try and catch your words, because your words indicate what you are thinking and your thoughts create your world."

How do we catch our words? By becoming more conscious, paying attention to our self-talk, and listening to our conversations with others.

A Simple Reminder ✳ Take Bowen's challenge to wear a special purple bracelet with the words "A Complaint Free World.org."

"You take the bracelet and every time you catch yourself complaining, you take it off one wrist, and you switch it over to the other wrist...and you keep doing it, back and forth, back and forth, until you go twenty-one consecutive days without complaining. Why twenty-one days? Scientists believe it takes twenty-one days to form a new habit," he says.

For the remainder of Lent, commit to maintaining a No Complaining Rule. If you don't like a situation, work to change it. If you can't change it, find a way to make peace with it. You can then be that burning and shining lamp, lighting the way for others to follow.

A Sincere Request ✳ *Dear Jesus, help me remember to keep my thoughts positive. Amen.*

WISDOM 2:1A, 12–22 • JOHN 7:1–2, 10, 25–30

If the Boot Doesn't Fit...

A kindergarten teacher was helping one of her students put on his boots. Even with her pulling and him pushing, the boots were slow to budge. When the second boot was finally on, she was nearly out of breath.

So they tried to arrest him, but no one laid a hand on him, because his hour had not yet come.

» JOHN 7:30

"They're on the wrong feet," the boy announced. The embarrassed teacher managed to keep her cool as she worked to pull both boots off and put them back on again.

Then the boy said, "These aren't my boots."

Once again, the teacher struggled to pull off the boots.

Then the boy said, "They're my brother's. Mom makes me wear them."

The teacher didn't know whether to laugh or cry. She mustered up the grace to wrestle the boots onto his feet again.

Finally, she said, "Now, where are your mittens?"

"I stuffed them in the toes of my boots," he said.

Patience. We need to practice it constantly. The setting of today's gospel is crucial because it's the final action-packed days as the clock ticks down toward the climax of Jesus' public ministry. Jesus showed extreme patience with the ambitious mother, in spite of all he had to face.

A Simple Reminder ✳ Create index cards with the quote "Please be patient. God hasn't finished with me yet!" Pass them out during Lent.

A Sincere Request ✳ *Dear Jesus, I'm always in a race against something. Give me the patience to relax and avoid the stress. Amen.*

Listening Is Caring!

One of my students was struggling with severe depression. More than once, she told her parents that she felt her world was caving in around her. They chose not to listen. When she finally did attempt suicide (without success, fortunately), her parents were dumbstruck. Can you imagine her frustration when they asked, "Why didn't you tell us you were having problems?"

My student could easily identify with Nicodemus when he responds to the Pharisees to "find out what Jesus is doing." We need to listen, really listen, to each other.

> *"Does our law condemn a person before it first hears him and finds out what he is doing?"*
>
> » JOHN 7:51

Some people, when they hear our first words, do two things: They stop listening and engage their mouths. They compose their comeback lines while we're still speaking, second-guess our thoughts, interrupt our words, try to finish our sentences, and dismiss our feelings.

And then there are the easy-listeners who engage their ears before their mouths. They seem to take our words seriously, connect to our feelings, and offer a shoulder for us to cry on.

Every day, we find ourselves slightly changed from the day before. If we fail to listen to others, one day we might find ourselves surrounded by total strangers who won't listen and who won't care.

A Simple Reminder ✳ Give three special gifts to your spouse, parent, or child: an open mind, an attentive ear, and an understanding heart.

A Sincere Request ✳ *Dear Jesus, help me learn to really listen and to think before I speak. Amen.*

Isaiah 43:16-21 • Philippians 3:8-14 • John 8:1-11
FOR YEAR A: Ezekiel 37:12-14 • Romans 8:8-11 • John 11:1-45 *or* 11:3-7, 17, 20-27, 33b-45

A Message in the Sand

I love the *Shrek* movies because of their clean humor and moral messages. Shrek, a no-nonsense ogre, has one major hang-up. He believes he should be alone because he's ugly. Many who see him agree without ever knowing what he's really like. Of course, by the end of each movie, everyone realizes how great he is on the inside. These films carry an important message: Take time to get to know someone before making judgments.

> *Jesus bent down and began to write...*
>
> » JOHN 8:6

Jesus comes face to face with an angry mob of Pharisees who need to learn that same lesson. But when Jesus bends down to write in the sand, he turns their world upside down. He forces them to admit to their own sinful behavior before condemning someone else.

Critics don't care about us. They prefer to humiliate us by remembering and recycling our mistakes. They prevent us from moving forward with our lives, exaggerate our flaws and shortcomings, stretch the truth, make up stories, spread rumors, and blow everything out of proportion.

Encouragers, on the other hand, show us how much they care. They liberate us from negative comments and wrongful judgments, persuade us to forgive ourselves, motivate us to move beyond our circumstances and appreciate the blessings in our lives, and awaken within us the desire to make positive changes by tapping into our hidden potential.

A Simple Reminder ✳ Be an encourager. Write notes to the encouragers who have set you free.

A Sincere Request ✳ *Dear Jesus, help me take a good look at myself before judging someone else. Amen.*

DANIEL 13:1–9, 15–17, 19–30, 33–62 *or* 13:41C–62 • JOHN 8:12–20

Explore Your Family Tree

I asked my students to write a short family history: information about their parents, grandparents, siblings, and any special moments they could remember. Many of them just stared at me blankly.

It quickly became apparent that they knew very little about their families. The meaning of Jesus' words today, "You know neither me nor my Father," resonates from what I discovered from my students.

> *"You know neither me nor my Father."*
>
> » JOHN 8:19

They felt great joy when they completed this assignment. For some, it was the best "together" time their family had spent in years.

Now they know about their mom's dreams as a young girl, their dad's most challenging dilemma, and the weirdest thing their sister ever did. One student said, "When I think that my parents could have died and I wouldn't have known these things, it really motivates me to learn more."

A Simple Reminder ✳ Explore your family tree! Encourage each member of your family to write about their experiences. Put their words into a scrapbook. Create a caption list for each page, such as: "Earliest childhood memories," "Best and worst teachers," "Games I played as a child," "My heroes and why I admire them," "Crazy teenage adventures," "Happiest heartfelt moments," "The worst thing that ever happened to me," "My relationship with God." Share your scrapbooks with one another. Pass them on to the next generation.

A Sincere Request ✳ *Dear Jesus, help me to stay connected to my family by asking questions and listening to their stories. Amen.*

Can You Hear God Now?

Most of us have seen the commercial where the cell phone guy stops every few feet and asks, "Can you hear me now?" When he gets his answer, he smiles and responds with a heartfelt "Good!" The service is accessible, reliable, and clear. Now, that's encouragement!

> *"I do nothing on my own."*
> » JOHN 8:28

Many of us would love to have that kind of positive feedback in our lives. But some of us live somewhere between dull discouragement and sheer panic, harassed by deadlines, bruised by worry, and broken by disillusionment.

We need someone to encourage us as we put the confusing pieces of our lives together. God is always there to motivate us with an inspired plan of action. God has blueprints for us to follow and heart prints for us to experience. We need to keep reminding ourselves: "I do nothing on my own."

Linger with God's words for a while. They are powerful and tailor-made for cloudy days. They can send a beam of light through the fog. Write down inspiring passages in a notebook. Call it: My Daily Dose of Encouragement.

A Simple Reminder ❋ Don't let encouraging words go unspoken. Write to your parents, best friends, and old friends long unseen but not forgotten. Thank them for nurturing you when you needed it most. Write to your favorite teachers and say, "Thanks for that blast of encouragement." Can you imagine what that might mean to them? Wouldn't you feel wonderful if you received that message from a friend or loved one?

A Sincere Request ❋ *Dear Jesus, sometimes I get discouraged, but I refuse to give up. Your loving presence always keeps me going. Amen.*

An Extreme Makeover

Quirks, foibles, compulsions, emotional hang-ups, and tons of baggage can keep us from feeling our happiness inside. Many of us have learned to accept our bad habits, rather than take the steps to correct them.

> *"So if a son frees you, then you will truly be free."*
>
> » JOHN 8:36

Here are three simple action steps we can take to experience our own transformation.

- First, admit that your behavior pushes people away and causes them to feel uncomfortable. Make a list of your offensive actions. Ask your friends to be candid and help you fill in the blanks.

- Second, knit together a strategy for managing your unpleasant conduct. Dig deep to find out what motivates you. Know the triggers (when, where, and with whom) that set off those unhealthy patterns within you.

- Third, quit doing those things. Practice regular maintenance to curb setbacks. If you catch yourself slipping, practice doing something positive.

Sometimes it's our constant negative comments that drive people crazy. Other times, it's our low self-esteem and our "woe is me" attitude that keeps them away. Whatever it is, we can change and "truly be free."

A Simple Reminder ✳ Check in regularly with counselors, sponsors, mentors, or support groups, and use these caring people as emotional compasses to guide and direct your growth. Stay positive. Don't give up.

....

A Sincere Request ✳ *Dear Jesus, help me recognize that my inner beauty radiates outward for all to see. Amen.*

GENESIS 17:3-9 • JOHN 8:51-59

When Words Get in the Way

An old man sat on the bus holding a bunch of fresh flowers. Across the aisle, a young girl's eyes kept wandering back to his beautiful bouquet. The man sensed that she was in pain. When he rose to get off the bus, he placed the flowers on her lap. "I feel that you need these," he said, "and I think my wife would like for you to have them. I'll tell her I gave them to you."

> *"But I do know him and I keep his word."*
>
> » JOHN 8:55

With tears, the girl accepted the flowers and watched the man step off the bus and walk through the gate of a nearby cemetery.

In today's gospel the master of the servant shows us that compassion is caring in action. Compassion asks us to go where it hurts, enter into places of pain, and share in brokenness, fear, and anguish.

We'll have many opportunities to offer compassion. There will be funerals to attend, divorced friends to encourage, and people facing the horror of disease. We need each other's warmth to survive, pick up the pieces, and move on, and sometimes that warmth takes the form of a kind word or a bunch of flowers.

A Simple Reminder ✳ To the person starved for compassion, a simple comment can send them soaring: "You look wonderful today!" or "I'm so glad you're here!" These words can have a huge impact on someone's life. People are hungry for something positive, encouraging, and refreshing. Start today.

A Sincere Request ✳ *Dear Jesus, my words can mend a broken life. Thank you for teaching me compassion. Help me find the right words when I need them. Amen.*

You've Crossed the Line!

"I'm the best thing that ever happened to you," Alex said emphatically. "No one else would put up with a slob like you."

Molly retaliated by saying, "Look who's calling me a slob. Stop by a mirror and take a long look at yourself."

This couple's relentless verbal abuse contaminated their relationship. The three of us finally sat down and looked for ways to create positive change.

They tried again to arrest him; but he escaped from their power.

» JOHN 10:39

Like this couple, we must establish strong boundaries. When someone ridicules us, we usually go into Red Alert. Instead, declare certain topics to be totally off-limits. Say, "These are my problems and not yours."

Don't allow people to affect your feelings or to define who you are with their negative comments. Firmly communicate to them that you will not be accepting or even acknowledging their criticism of you any longer. Standing your ground and setting boundaries are ways to honor and respect yourself. You escape from their power.

A Simple Reminder ✳ Complete the following statements:
- "People may no longer..."
- "I have a right to ask for..."
- "To protect my time and energy, it's OK to..."

Finish each sentence with at least six examples of boundaries you can set to honor yourself. Select the easiest ones and start communicating them to those who need to hear them.

A Sincere Request ✳ *Dear Jesus, help me forgive those who've crossed the line and hurt me. Give me the courage to stand my ground and express my truth. Amen.*

Cherish the Little Things!

When I think about my mother, the first image that comes to mind is me holding her hand at my brother-in-law's funeral. That was six weeks before she died. I had never really noticed how beautiful her hands were until I saw them that day, really for the first and last time, entwined in mine.

> *Many...who had...seen what he had done began to believe in him.*
>
> » JOHN 11:45

Significant moments are small things that are forgotten when life gets complicated and hectic. Our genuine, real, authentic selves hide in the little things that we've forgotten. The big moments, like the wedding, the baby, the new house, and the dream job, are just the punctuation marks of our personal memories. Our stories are written every day in the small, simple, and common moments.

Give yourself a small-things-forgotten day to rediscover the significant moments that have influenced your life. Rediscover the books, movies, clothes, photos, furnishings, pets, and playthings that were significant in your life. Re-experience the vacations, the color of a flower or sunset, or a song on the radio. Remember people, events, comforts, comic strips, music, and magazines that touched your heart. These are the small things that have a significant and special meaning for you.

Take time to discover, and then cherish, your small forgotten things.

A Simple Reminder ✳ What little things are you taking with you from your life? Select one today, with care, and appreciate it.

A Sincere Request ✳ *Dear Jesus, keep my eyes open to all the significant possibilities right under my nose. Amen.*

Beyond Betrayal

I had the rare privilege recently of meeting a rather spunky woman who was over one hundred years old. I couldn't resist asking her, "Of all the experiences you've had, what has been the most interesting?"

"The hand of the one who is to betray me is with me on the table."

» LUKE 22:21

Her answer shocked me. The most interesting, the defining moment in this beautiful woman's life, was when she caught her husband and her best friend together. She's lived over one hundred years, and this is her most significant memory. Such is the power of betrayal!

Each of us has probably felt betrayed by someone we've trusted. When working with people who have been betrayed, I've noticed that many move through the same emotional process: *Surprise:* "I can't believe this happened!" *Seclusion:* "Who needs people? They just let you down." *Sorry:* "I should have listened to so-and-so." *Sore:* "I'm so angry, I could..." *Seething:* "I'll get even someday." *Soothe:* "I want to be free from the pain."

Jesus knew all about betrayal, yet he was able to forgive.

Choosing to continue a relationship after betrayal requires more than just "I'm sorry" or "I forgive you." It demands rolling up your sleeves and rebuilding—with time, talk, and tenderness—the trust that was lost.

A Simple Reminder ✷ If you've been betrayed, surround yourself with supportive people. Interact with at least one positive person each day. Do something to show love for yourself every day. You will have some difficult moments. Allow them to pass. Healing takes time.

A Sincere Request ✷ *Dear Jesus, you know what I go through when people let me down. I want to trust again, and with your help, I will. Amen.*

41

ISAIAH 42:1-7 • JOHN 12:1-11

A Lifetime Commitment

Albert was restless and didn't know why. He was financially secure and had a nice home, but he didn't feel that he was living a meaningful life.

He said, "After Mass one Sunday, I reflected on my situation and compared it to others who seemed happy. Then it dawned on me! They do things that make a difference in the world. Their lives are all about service. At that moment, I made a commitment to do the same. That was over five years ago, and I can't begin to tell you the difference this has made in my life!"

> *"Mary took a liter of costly perfumed oil... and anointed the feet of Jesus."*
> » JOHN 12:3

A few days before Jesus' death, at a dinner in the house of a friend, Mary anointed his dusty feet using a flask of choice perfume. Our greatest challenge is to become other-centered. This opening of our hearts to others is the ultimate act of kindness.

It's easy to be kind. It can even be contagious. Decide to offer kindness every hour of every day. Make it a lifetime commitment.

A Simple Reminder ✳ Decide to do a kindness checklist. Begin with:

Family: Do something for your parents—fetch a blanket, clean off the table, or prepare the coffee—without being asked.

Workplace: Sit with a grumpy employee who is being avoided. Pay attention as he or she talks. Just be there and listen.

School: Invite some new students to your table who don't fit in. Talk to them and help them feel welcome.

A Sincere Request ✳ *Dear Jesus, help me to recognize opportunities where I can be kind to others. Amen.*

ISAIAH 49:1-6 • JOHN 13:21-33, 36-38

When the Bottom Falls Out

Barry arrived home one day to find that his wife had left him and taken the children with her. Now, as time drags on, Barry has only memories to warm him during the endless hours of loneliness. He asks: "God, is there no end to the hurt?"

Jesus was deeply troubled.

» JOHN 13:21

When hopes are shattered, don't give up. Look for ways to find some measure of relief. These three suggestions may help:

Cry it out. Let the tears flow. Trembling is acceptable. As you feel the pain empty out of your body, you will begin to heal.

Talk it out. Hurting people often say, "I can't talk about it," but you need to connect with other people and engage in heart-to-heart conversations. You'll gain insight and understanding into overlooked possibilities.

Write it out. If you're angry at God, that's OK. Get those deep hurts out. Resentment, hatred, envy, and vengeance are emotions that cause radioactive fallout that can gnaw at your health. Let these feelings go and write down all your negative thoughts in a journal.

When the bottom falls out and you can't find anything to grab onto, stop pretending that you have it all together and admit that you are hurting. Jesus did! Jesus will walk alongside you and will give you the reassurance and reinforcement you need to continue on. He's no stranger to feeling "troubled."

A Simple Reminder ✳ When life troubles you and turns you upside down, remember: This, too, shall pass.

A Sincere Request ✳ *Dear Jesus, allow me believe that nothing will happen today that I can't handle with your help. Amen.*

ISAIAH 50:4–9A • MATTHEW 26:14–25

Take a Ride with Forgiveness

A man was looking through the classified ads when he noticed a new Porsche for sale, in mint condition with low mileage, for only $50. When he saw the car, it was just as described. He promptly paid the $50.

Before he left, he asked the seller, "Why are you selling it for only $50?"

The woman replied, "My husband had an affair with another woman. He didn't have the courage to tell me to my face. Instead, he just left a note that said: 'I'm leaving you. You can keep the house and the kids. Just sell my Porsche and send me the money.' So, that's exactly what I'm doing."

Then Judas, his betrayer, said in reply, "Surely it is not I, Rabbi?"

» MATTHEW 26:25

Anyone who has ever been betrayed would probably give her a "high-five" for getting even with her husband. But while seeking revenge may seem satisfying, it's not all that helpful in the long run. It keeps us glued to anger and focused on resentment, and it prevents us from experiencing peace.

Make the decision to forgive. Let go of the past, the pain, and the sorrow, or continue to be worn down by bitterness and retaliation.

It hurts deeply to have been betrayed. Forgiving someone doesn't mean we pretend the betrayal never happened. Forgiving doesn't instantly make everything all right. Instead, we simply decide to no longer make the betrayal the predominant thought in our life. We move on by finding other, more joyful things to focus on.

A Simple Reminder ✳ Put on some soothing music and write out your emotions. You'll be surprised at how much better you will feel.

A Sincere Request ✳ *Dear Jesus, when you were betrayed, you forgave. Help me to do the same. This is the only way for me to move forward. Amen.*

44

CHRISM MASS: ISAIAH 61:1–3A, 6A, 8B–9 • REVELATION 1:5–8 • LUKE 4:16–21
EVENING MASS OF THE LORD'S SUPPER: EXODUS 12:1–8, 11–14 •
1 CORINTHIANS 11:23–26 • JOHN 13:1–15

Do the Unexpected

One day, Caroline, a struggling single mom, learned that she had only thirty days to either buy the house she lived in or face eviction.

Her friend Veronica felt compelled to call Caroline that very day, just to say hello. That one phone call changed their lives forever.

> *"You ought to wash one another's feet."*
> » JOHN 13:14

"It was clear she'd been crying," Veronica later explained, "and she told me the news. I knew that what happened to her could happen to any of us."

A simple plan was hatched that day that saved Caroline's home.

On this holy night, we find Jesus washing the feet of others. This humble act reminds us to help the helpless, serve the lonely, and rescue those (like Caroline) who are in despair.

As we come together to dine on this special night, we may feel Jesus gently nudge us to leave our churches and immerse ourselves into the lives of hungry, helpless people.

As foot washers, we can do the unexpected. We can serve people well, cheerfully, and out of the limelight. When this happens, the day often comes when they smile and say, "I'm full."

A Simple Reminder ✳ The world is in great need of helpers. Make time each day to reach out to someone. Do something unexpected for a friend, even if it's simply making a phone call. You just might change a life forever.

....

A Sincere Request ✳ *Dear Jesus, when I offer to help others, I'm really helping you and myself. Nudge me to do that every day. Amen.*

ISAIAH 52:13—53:12 • HEBREWS 4:14-16; 5:7-9 • JOHN 18:1—19:42

What Will Matter?

John's wife always wanted to visit her relatives in Poland, the country where her parents were born. It was her only wish.

Even though he could afford the trip, John thought it was a frivolous way to spend money. There were always car and house payments to make, groceries to buy, and savings needed for the children's college fund.

"It is finished."
» JOHN 19:30

Today, the house and car are paid for, food is still on the table, and the children are educated, married, and have moved on with families of their own. John's wife passed away last year without ever having realized her dream. If only he had listened.

I hear it so many times when a loved one dies: "If I had a second chance to live life over, I would do things so differently."

Once we've lived these days, they are gone forever. If we could see just five minutes beyond death, we'd know how we should be living, right now. A hundred years from now, it will not matter what our bank balance was, the kind of house we lived in, or the type of car we drove. What will matter will be the times we said, "I love you," "Thank you," or "I'm sorry." What will matter will be the moments when we treated people with tenderness, compassion, love, and respect.

A Simple Reminder ✷ Avoid putting things off, making excuses, or wasting precious time. Turn off your voice mail, phone, TV, and computer. Be deliberate about spending time with the people you love. Remember to listen, hug, and say "I love you" while you still have the chance.

A Sincere Request ✷ *Dear Jesus, remind me to live, love, and laugh, now and in every moment. Amen.*

GENESIS 1:1—2:2 *or* 1:1, 26–31A • GENESIS 22:1–18 *or* 22:1-2, 9A, 10–13, 15–18 •
EXODUS 14:15—15:1 • ISAIAH 54:5-14 • ISAIAH 55:1-11 • BARUCH 3:9-15, 32—4:4 •
EZEKIEL 36:16-17A, 18–28 • ROMANS 6:3-11 • LUKE 24:1-12

A Fresh Start!

Stephen confessed that he had recently hurt someone and felt terrible about it: "All I want is to be forgiven," he said. "I just can't live with the guilt."

One of the hardest things to do is to let go. We are our own chief tormentor. Harboring resentment, holding grudges, or focusing on blame only hurts us. We have to move on and stop wasting valuable energy on the past.

"Remember what he said to you while he was still in Galilee."

» LUKE 24:6

Easter is for forgiveness, compassion, and understanding. By changing the way we think, we can turn regret and worry into distant memories.

It's never too late to start over. I don't care how low we go or where we've been: failure is never final unless we let it be.

The message of Easter is this: Jesus doesn't care about what we've done or our permanent record. What matters is the direction of our feet right now and where we are headed. We shouldn't dwell on the past or continue to beat ourselves up over it. We can't change it, and we don't have to. We can, however, live differently from this day forward.

A Simple Reminder ✳ Forgive those who have harmed you. If you have hurt another, sincerely apologize. Then, regardless of their reaction, take a deep breath and let go. Ask for a fresh start. Find any thought that helps you feel better. Find something to focus on that brings some measure of relief. Make a decision to be happy, no matter what. The fastest way to let go of your past is to concentrate on those things in your life now that bring you joy.

A Sincere Request ✳ *Dear Jesus, help me find the determination to pick myself up and start over. Amen.*

LITURGICAL CALENDAR
for LENT 2025

MARCH

5	WED	**ASH WEDNESDAY**
6	THU	Thursday after Ash Wednesday
7	FRI	Friday after Ash Wednesday
		Sts. Perpetua and Felicity
8	SAT	Saturday after Ash Wednesday
		St. John of God
9	SUN	**FIRST SUNDAY OF LENT**
10	MON	Lenten Weekday
11	TUE	Lenten Weekday
12	WED	Lenten Weekday
13	THU	Lenten Weekday
14	FRI	Lenten Weekday
15	SAT	Lenten Weekday
16	SUN	**SECOND SUNDAY OF LENT**
17	MON	Lenten Weekday
		St. Patrick
18	TUE	Lenten Weekday
		St. Cyril of Jerusalem
19	WED	**ST. JOSEPH**
20	THU	Lenten Weekday
21	FRI	Lenten Weekday
22	SAT	Lenten Weekday
23	SUN	**THIRD SUNDAY OF LENT**
24	MON	Lenten Weekday
25	TUE	**THE ANNUNCIATION OF THE LORD**
26	WED	Lenten Weekday
27	THU	Lenten Weekday
28	FRI	Lenten Weekday
29	SAT	Lenten Weekday
30	SUN	**FOURTH SUNDAY OF LENT**
31	MON	Lenten Weekday

APRIL

1	TUE	Lenten Weekday
2	WED	Lenten Weekday
		St. Francis of Paola
3	THU	Lenten Weekday
4	FRI	Lenten Weekday
		St. Isidore
5	SAT	Lenten Weekday
		St. Vincent Ferrer
6	SUN	**FIFTH SUNDAY OF LENT**
7	MON	Lenten Weekday
		St. John Baptist de la Salle
8	TUE	Lenten Weekday
9	WED	Lenten Weekday
10	THU	Lenten Weekday
11	FRI	Lenten Weekday
		St. Stanislaus
12	SAT	Lenten Weekday
13	SUN	**PALM SUNDAY OF THE PASSION OF THE LORD**
14	MON	Monday of Holy Week
15	TUE	Tuesday of Holy Week
16	WED	Wednesday of Holy Week
17	THU	**HOLY THURSDAY**
18	FRI	**GOOD FRIDAY**
19	SAT	**HOLY SATURDAY**
20	SUN	**EASTER SUNDAY OF THE RESURRECTION OF THE LORD**

COURTESY OF
Living with Christ
YOUR DAILY COMPANION FOR
PRAYING AND LIVING THE EUCHARIST
www.livingwithchrist.us

ISBN 978-1-62785-830-4

TWENTY-THIRD PUBLICATIONS

977 Hartford Turnpike, Unit A; Waterford, CT 06385
twentythirdpublications.com

9 781627 858304

bayard

Lent 2025

DAILY MEDITATIONS, ACTIONS & PRAYERS

LIVING *with* PASSION